THE WHITENESS

OF

BIRCH

99 Haiku

Frank Kaczmarek

LIBRARY OF CONGRESS
CATALOGING-IN-PUBLICATION DATA

Kaczmarek Frank.
The Whiteness of Birch / Frank Kaczmarek

Cover photographs
by Frank Kaczmarek
Natural Lines Photography

ISBN 9781936711543

10 9 8 7 6 5 4 3 2 1

Railroad Street Press
394 Railroad St., Ste 2
St. Johnsbury, VT 05819

For the grandkids:

Maddyson
Landon
Camdyn

Spring

cascade-
stone gives voice
to water

spring thaw-
river ice flows
on ice

creeping in from
the windowsill's corner-
moonlight

leaping off a cliff
a falcon assumes
its shape

early spring rains-
among faded leaves
the brightness of moss

downpour-
tree bark darkens
the rain

dappled sunlight
drifting through the forest
newborn fawn

overnight shower-
now inching up the mountain
morning mist

after the rain
sunshine unravels
a lily

in the storm's wake
the forest restores
stillness

slowly growing
into the earth
old gravestones

shrouded in fog-
only the mourning dove's hoot
betrays its presence

in the tall treetops
lingering with the crows
twilight

first sign of spring–
a carpenter ant
shares my kitchen

deep in a pool
within a pool of shadow–
trout

loitering among
the streambed stones
trout shadows

a hawk's cry
its open beak carries
only sky

the child tries hard
to recall the flower's name-
forget-me-not

spring breeze-
marsh reeds rustle
with birdsong

evening heat-
between fireflies
lightning

abandoned orchard-
weaving through the weeds
scent of apple blossoms

turning
into the mist
the unnamed stream

sunrise-
the yellow
of spring

dawn's hued crescendo
the changing play of light
on fiddleheads

Summer

rolling off a leaf
a dewdrop carries
away the sun

as I pass
the dragonfly returns
to the same perch

summer heat-
under a fallen leaf
a toad finds shade

summer afternoon-
paddling the canoe
through cloudswirl

water's edge-
a moose drinks
her reflection

morning light-
lake and sky blend
with each paddle stroke

loon's cry-
on the lake floats
an eagle's shadow

tongue flicking
a garter snake smells the air
smells me

loon's call-
from across the lake
only echoes answer

windblown cattails-
a heron stands
motionless

butterfly hunting
my granddaughter's hands
encircle emptiness

sinking deeper
into the wet grass
the snail's path

daybreak-
in front of the bulldozer
the snail's path

moonrise-
slowly crossing the stream
tree shadows

lost
in the surrounding shade
my shadow

summer storm
entering the lake
raindrops

calm lake-
I submerge myself behind
a tree's reflection

thunderstorm-
torrential rains wet
the sea

campfire-
the bright glow of
children's faces

after days of rain
the sucking sounds of boots
pull loose the mud

heat wave-
only the breeze rippled grass
moves

for a brief time
the old white fence painted pink-
setting sun

dawn-
the empty window
fills with sunlight

old field-
clover engulfed in
the hum of bees

dropping deep
into the corn field
the crow's caw

cautiously eyeing
the molting spider
she sheds her phobia

at the water's edge
a lone heron becomes two-
windless morning

picture window–
a wasp flits from
cloud to cloud

tundra sky
a dark cloud lifts into it–
mosquitoes

overcast sky–
my shadow and I now
occupy the same space

early morning hike
the woodland trail blocked-
spider's web

rising
with the rising sun
forest scents

rumble of thunder
all along the ridgeline
quaking aspens

approaching storm-
sky and sea begin to change
but always sky and sea

in a forest
devoid of forest
clear-cut

after the rainstorm
into the soil seeps streams
of sunlight

Autumn

hunter's moon-
geese pierce
the light

back at home recalling
the physician's prognosis-
hard frost

autumn dawn-
dragonfly shapes
the dew

fallen leaves-
rain catches
rain

no longer certain
which path to take-
autumn fog

drenching rain-
the bent heads
of indian pipes

autumn breezes
in and out of the valley
cloud shadows

campfire-
skimming across tree trunks
my shadow

inside a curled leaf
a spider waits patiently-
midday shower

hanging
just above the campfire
night's blackness

slowly retreating
in the early morning sun
last night's frost

dusk-
lost in the forest
the sky's colors

autumn wind
the deer's fur ripples-
maggots

deer carcass-
the rising stench
of flies

persistent drizzle-
overnight the decaying log
becomes mushroom

rotting apples
their odor fills the air
with wasps

single yellow leaf
drops, rises, drops again-
october breezes

cloud's passing shadow
alters the forest
leaving it unaltered

nature walk-
a deer vanishes into
the click of the shutter

from deep within
a trumpet flower
the bee's buzzzzz

autumn ballooning
letting the wind take the lead-
spiderlings

autumn haze-
my mother remembering
......not remembering

late autumn hike-
aster blooms tinged with
the scent of decay

dense fog
the mountain peaks
buried in sky

Winter

the boy following
in his father's footsteps-
winter hike

five o'clock cocktail-
watching the young woman
adjust the I.V.

blizzard whiteout-
winds gust out of nowhere
into nowhere

storm's end–
the old graveyard
buried in snow

fallen snow–
the whiteness
of birch

winter winds–
the empty sky fills with
the creaking of trees

winter woods-
tree branches hold
only sky

the brightness of dust
on the windowsill-
winter sun

low winter sun-
stretched across the cornfield
afternoon shadows

pausing to balance
at the top of a pine tree-
full moon

mountain home-
welcoming the fire
welcoming the wood

birch trees
still white against
the snow

january thaw–
into the valley flows
fog

flurries–
just enough snow
mouse tracks

mountain silence–
snow falling on
fallen snow

ABOUT THE AUTHOR

Frank Kaczmarek and his wife, Colleen, live in Lyman, NH. His previous book, <u>New England Wildflowers: a guide to common plants,</u> was published by Globe-Pequot Press, Guilford, CT in 2009.